WEIRDO 9
SPOOKY WEIRD!

Scholastic Press
An imprint of Scholastic Australia Pty Limited (ABN 11 000 614 577)
PO Box 579 Gosford NSW 2250
www.scholastic.com.au

Part of the Scholastic Group
Sydney • Auckland • New York • Toronto • London • Mexico City
• New Delhi • Hong Kong • Buenos Aires • Puerto Rico

First published by Scholastic Australia in 2017.

NATIONAL LIBRARY
A catalogue record for this book is available from the National Library of Australia

ISBN: 978-93-5471-866-3

Typeset in Grenadine MVB, Push Ups and Lunch Box.

This reprint edition: February, 2025

Printed in India

BLAH, BLAH, BLAH

ANH DO

Illustrated by JULES FABER

WEIRDO 9

SPOOKY WEIRD!

A SCHOLASTIC PRESS BOOK
FROM SCHOLASTIC AUSTRALIA

BOO!

CHAPTER 1

I love Halloween. It's **so much fun** dressing up in costumes and walking around the neighborhood with **your friends**.

Henry always wears something that makes me **laugh**. Like the time he dressed up as a **tree**.

OH NO, STOP THAT!

Last year, Henry dressed up as a **target**.

It was **great** until we walked past some people doing **archery!**

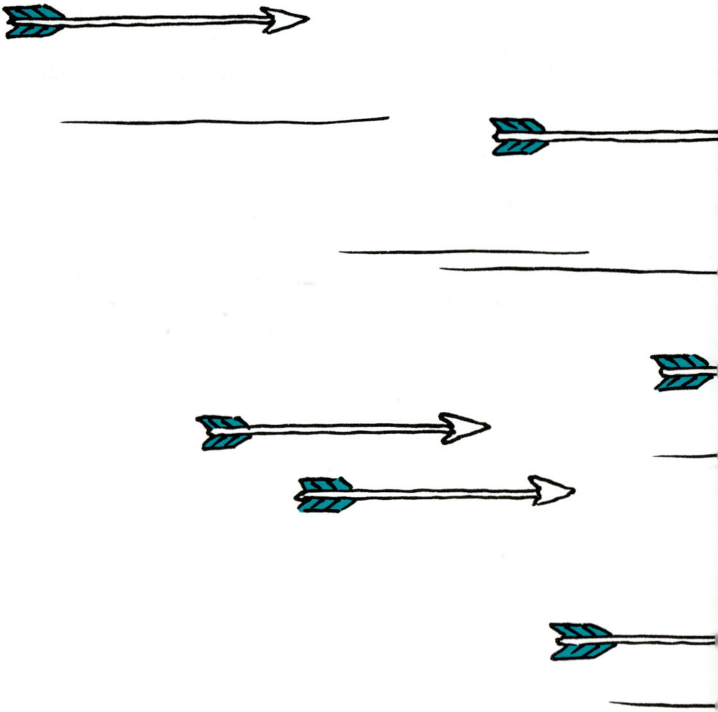

But there's **one** thing about Halloween that's even better than Henry's **funny** costumes . . .

LOLLIES!

It's the **one night** of the year where grown-ups hand out lollies **everywhere** you look!

Even the **dentist** gives out lollies!

I love lollies that look like **false teeth**. We all pretend to be just like Granddad!

In school, Miss Franklin was planning **trick-or-treating** for our class. First, we had to pair up for craft time—we were going to make our own Halloween **costumes!**

Miss Franklin pointed to Wendy...

'Mullet,' she said, 'you team up with Clare. And **Bella** . . . You go with—'

Hans Some and I were sitting up **REALLY** straight, to get noticed. We **both** wanted to be chosen to pair up with **Bella!**

'Bella,' Miss Franklin said, 'you go with **Weir.'**

Awesome!

Bella reached over and we **high-fived.**

It was going to be **heaps of fun** making them together.

Once I made a **MUMMY** costume out of **toilet paper . . .**

. . . but after it **rained** I looked like I'd been

FLUSHED down the toilet!

My **Bag of Chips Vending Machine** costume was pretty cool, though!

In fact, it was a **HUGE HIT!**

MINE!
CHIPS!
OOH!
YUM!
MMM!
CHIPS!
YUM!
SALT AND VINEGAR!
MY FAVOURITE!

But somehow I had to **TOP** that and come up with something

completely new

and

completely

AWESOME!

THE BLOBS!

CHAPTER 2

After school, Bella and I were walking home to my place. We were going to get started on our **Halloween costumes!**

'What about a pair of **zombies**?' said Bella. 'Or **mad scientists**?'

'Or an **astronaut**?' I suggested.

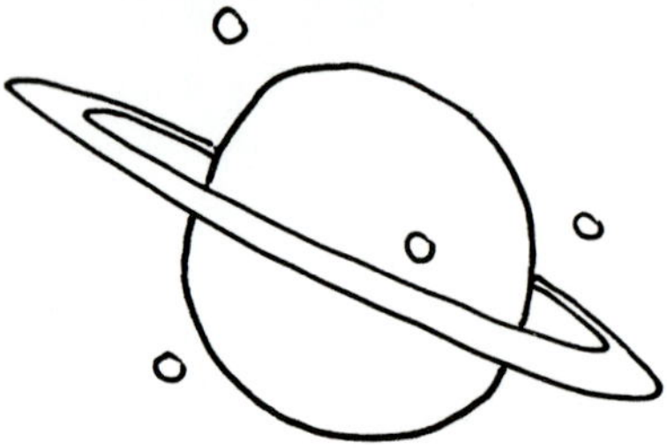

WHY DID THE ASTRONAUT'S TRIP TO **MARS** GO **WRONG**?

HE DIDN'T **PLANET** PROPERLY!

'Hey, look,' said Bella, pointing to a **sign** on a telegraph pole.

'I hope they find her,' said Bella.

'Me too,' I agreed. **'Poor Molly.'**

As we neared my house, we saw **Blockhead** and **FiDo** at the front door.

'What if we **dressed up** as Blockhead and FiDo?' I said to Bella.

'That would be **so funny!**' said Bella, laughing. 'But they'd be **pretty hard** costumes to make!'

Bella was right. Those ideas wouldn't be **easy!**

Plus we had to find materials. The first thing we had to do was see what kind of **stuff** we could find in the **garage**.

We said **hello** to Blockhead and FiDo, but they barely gave us a **woof**. In fact, they both looked **really sad.**

Inside the house,

it didn't get

any

better!

'What's going on?' I asked.

WHY DO YOU ALL LOOK **SO SAD?**

No-one said anything right away . . .
but then Sally **spoke up.**

WE'RE
MOVING HOUSE,
WEIR . . .

MOVING?
WHAT DO
YOU MEAN?

What was Sally talking about?!

She looked like she might **cry!**

'We're **moving away**!' said Sally with a sniffle.

Mum and Dad sat me down and told me that Sally was right. That we – **the Do family** – were moving away!

I couldn't **believe** it!

But why?

Mum and Dad explained that we needed to **move out** of our house and **find another one** . . . but the problem was, they couldn't find anything nearby that they could afford.

So they had no choice but to move us to a **new place** that was really **FAR away!**

We had to **change schools** and everything!

'But I don't want to leave,' I said. 'I **love** our house, our street, my school . . .'

And then I looked at *Bella*.

'And my **FRIENDS!'**

'I don't want to live **anywhere** but here!' I said.

Anywhere else would feel like another **planet**!

'When?' I asked. 'When do we have to move?'

'I'm sorry, Weir,' said Mum, 'but we have to pack up and leave **next week**.'

This was **the worst news ever.**

BATH MAN!

CHAPTER 3

We couldn't find **anything** in the garage that we could use to make our **Halloween costumes.**

Bella was searching **everywhere** . . . but I was too busy thinking about how I'd be moving away so soon . . .

It would be my **last** Halloween with my friends!

A cloud of dust rose as Bella picked up two towels and **shook** them.

Once the dust settled, Bella said,

'Superhero capes?'

'Whenever there are **wet** people who need **drying**—we'll be there!' I said.

'Hmm, maybe not,' said Bella.

'What about these?' said Bella, picking up a few pairs of Mum's **old stockings**.

We'd need **WAY** more legs than that!

'There's nothing useful here,' I said. 'Maybe I shouldn't bother going **trick-or-treating** ...'

Bella looked a bit disappointed, but then she **spotted** something in the corner.

'We just have to look **harder!'** she said. 'We can turn **anything** into a costume!'

NOW I'M
A TURTLE!

AND THIS
OLD UMBRELLA?

NOW I'M
A BAT!

Bella pulled out one of Sally's old **hula hoops.**

NOW I'M SATURN!

UHH . . .

Next, Bella began wriggling into Granddad's **sleeping bag**.

She was thinking hard. What was she going to come up with next? **A burrito?**

A **sleeping bag?!**

Bella's ideas were **TERRIBLE!**

But they were also
pretty funny!

Bella laughed too and started **wobbling**!

'Uh-oh, I think I'm stuck!' she said, losing her balance.

BUMP!

Bella **tipped** over and **bumped** a shelf by the wall. At that moment, something from way up top **fell right on my head.**

'What's that?' asked Bella, getting up and looking a bit **dizzy!**

I brushed the dust off the bag that had fallen on **me**.

'They're just a big old bag of **green balloons** . . .' I said, tossing them aside.

Our garage search had given us **NOTHING** to use for our Halloween costumes! We needed to come up with **another plan**.

'Hi guys!' said Dad, popping his head in the garage.

He was carrying a **big bowl** of grapes. **Green** and **round** and **juicy**. 'Want a snack?'

'Thanks, Dad,' I said, as Bella and I **helped ourselves** to a bunch each.

They were **delicious.**

And then suddenly it **hit us!**

'We can use the **BALLOONS** to make us look like bunches of **GRAPES!**' I said, high-fiving Bella.

WHAT A GRAPE IDEA!

MR MEAN!

CHAPTER 4

It can be pretty fun when you get to take a day off school . . . But **NOT** when your granddad's taking you to **SEE YOUR NEW SCHOOL!**

The one that's **far, far away!**

Granddad left me at **my new class**, then went away to take Sally to hers.

My new teacher's name was **Mr Lean**.

He had these **big furry** eyebrows that made him look **REALLY** cranky!

More like **Mr Mean!**

Anyone could look mean with those!

Mr Mean – I mean, **Mr Lean** – looked at me.

'And what's your name?' he asked.

I was about to tell him **the truth** about my name, but I didn't want him to **laugh at me**. So I made something up.

There! That was better than admitting my name was **WEIRDO!**

But **guess what** the teacher did next?

He rolled around the floor **LAUGHING!**

'What's your brother's name?' he said. **'Fear Some!?** Or your mum – **Awe Some?!'**

'And what about your dad?' said Mr Mean.

By now, the **whole class** was laughing.

**BA-HA HA HA HA
HA HA HA HA!**

If they all thought **HANS SOME** was a funny name . . . what were they going to think of **WEIR DO?!**

Finally, Mr Lean stopped laughing and introduced me to the class.

There was . . .

Blair
Coby Hogan
Benny
and Stella Allen

Plus there was a kid who looked
just like the **REAL** Hans Some . . .
His name was

Goode Looking!

I was **so busy** trying to look cool, like the **real** Hans Some, I forgot I was wearing

my dad's

old shoes . . .

and

tripped!

I'd done it **again!**

This new school **WAS NOT** off to a great start!

SNIFF!

CHAPTER 5

'I don't think *that* school is right for me,' I told Mum and Dad later that night. 'It was **really weird**.'

Mum kept telling me it would get better. And that I'd settle in **REALLY QUICKLY** and make new friends in **NO TIME**.

But I didn't want to **settle** in.

I didn't want to make **new** friends.

I just wanted to keep the friends I already had!

Even **Blockhead** and **FiDo** were sad about the move.

They **loved exploring** our street, and playing **games** in our house. But just like us, they had boxes that needed to be packed.

I had just **one day** left at **MY** school . . . then it was Halloween . . . and then we'd be packing up our place and leaving **for good**.

My last day at school wasn't easy. I would miss this place so much!

I'd miss Toby always **dropping things**...

I'd miss Henry **making me laugh**...

I'd even miss those birds in the playground that were always **pooping on my head!**

I was feeling **pretty sad** as I walked into my classroom after lunch. The day had gone **so fast!** I only had a couple of hours to go . . .

The classroom was **empty.**

WHERE IS EVERYONE?

SURPRISE!
WE'LL
MISS

YOU, WEIRDO!

It turns out Bella had organised a **huge goodbye party** for me!

Miss Franklin had even made a cake that looked just like **me**!

I slowly made my way around class, saying **goodbye** to everyone.

Even **Blake Green** was nice to me.

Saying goodbye to Henry and Bella was going to be **the hardest**. Luckily I was going to see them again later for **Trick-or-Treating.**

We **promised** we'd **write** to each other all the time! And **visit** as much as possible!

Henry even sang me a **farewell poem**.

THERE ONCE WAS A BOY
CALLED WEIRDO.
YES, HIS NAME WAS WEIR,
OH!
HE MAKES US
LAUGH,
HE'S A CLOWN-
AND-A-HALF,

THAT'S WHY HE'S MY FRIEND AND MY HERO!

GO
AWAY!

CHAPTER 6

On our way to my house, to finish off our **GRAPE** costumes, Bella and I stopped by the place **next** to hers.

There was a **FOR RENT** sign in the yard, almost covered by bushes and weeds.

'Oh, that place is **super SPOOKY**,' said Bella. 'No-one wants to move in there . . .'

'But why?' I asked.

. . . BECAUSE IT'S HAUNTED!

'Come on, Bella, you don't believe that stuff, do you?' I asked.

She didn't answer, but gave me a look that said maybe she **DID** believe it.

Bella told me there were **strange noises** coming out of the house . . . and that no-one lived in there, but lately people swore they could hear **voices** coming from inside.

'I think people must be **imagining** things,' I said, trying to sound confident.

Just then, we heard a **REALLY SPOOOOOOKY** voice call out from inside.

GO AWAY!
DO NOT ENTER!
WOOOOO

'Did you just hear that?' said Bella, looking panicked.

Before I could answer, we heard the voice again!

'GO AWAY!' it hissed. **'WOOOOO!'**

It didn't need to tell us twice! We **bolted!**

AHHHH!

AHHHHHH

That place **really is** haunted,' I said.

'Told you so!' said Bella.

We were both **so relieved** to be at my house and away from that **creepy place!**

Besides, we had work to do. We had **hundreds** of **balloons** to blow up for our **grape costumes!**

There were just **SO MANY** balloons!

It was taking us **forever!**

But finally, Bella blew up the **very last** balloon.

With Mum's help, we attached the balloons to our clothes. Lastly, she put **two old green hats** on our heads, which looked like **leaves**!

We were ready to **TRICK OR TREAT!**

KNOCK, KNOCK!

CHAPTER 7

Henry and Wendy were waiting outside to meet us.

'You make a great **witch**, Wendy!' said Bella.

'Yeah, and that's a cool **ghost** costume,' I said to Henry.

I was going to miss Henry's jokes!

Henry and Wendy loved our **grape** costumes. I reached out to shake Henry's hand.

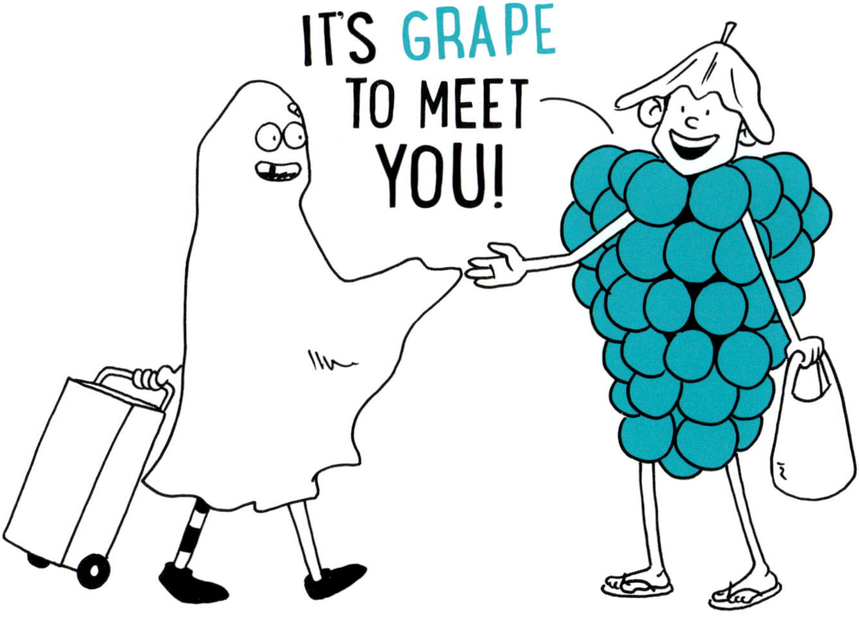

'Don't forget to knock on **our** door!' Mum called out. We turned and wandered back up the path to her.

We all **sang** out . . .

TRICK OR TREAT!

Mum and Dad dropped something **BIG** into our bags!

We were going to have a **HUGE** night, if this was how much we were going to get from **every house!**

We reached into our bags to find out what we'd been given.

I fished out something long. Maybe a **chocolate bar?!**

But it **wasn't** a chocolate bar.

And Henry fished out something else.

'Thanks Mr and Mrs Do,' said Bella, politely.

Just as we were about to head off in search of **REAL LOLLIES**, Blockhead flew out of the house to join us!

ARRRR-MATEY!

'I couldn't help it,' said Mum. 'I made him a **little costume** too!'

I looked at my friends. **'Let's go!'**

We had one of the **greatest nights** together.

We

talked and

laughed . . .

. . . we ran into **other people from school . . .**

Like Mullet . . .

dressed as a **mullet**!

And James Nott . . .

dressed as a **runny nose**!

We saw some **really WEIRD** costumes too . . .

. . . and we collected lollies!

Loads of **LOLLIES!**

This was our **biggest haul EVER!**

After we were done for the night, we said our **goodbyes**. Henry and Wendy went one way and Bella and I went another. I was going to walk her home.

'Thanks for a **grape** night, you guys,' Henry called out. 'Don't stay out too long or you'll turn into **sultanas**!'

The house next to Bella's was even **spookier**-looking tonight.

Bella and I **jumped** as we heard a tiny murmur, coming from inside.

'It was nothing,' said Bella. 'Don't worry.'

But then we heard it **again!**

'Go away!' a spooky voice hissed. **'Go away!'**

Blockhead suddenly **squawked** and **flapped** and **flew off!** He was heading right for the **house!**

'Blockhead, no!' I shouted. 'Come back!'

But it was too late! He'd flown through an open window, right into the **HAUNTED HOUSE!**

'What do we do now?' I asked Bella.

'We go in after him, I guess . . .' she said, walking towards the gate.

Man, she was brave!

WAY

braver

than me!

I was so scared, all my balloons were **shaking!**

EEEEEEEEK!

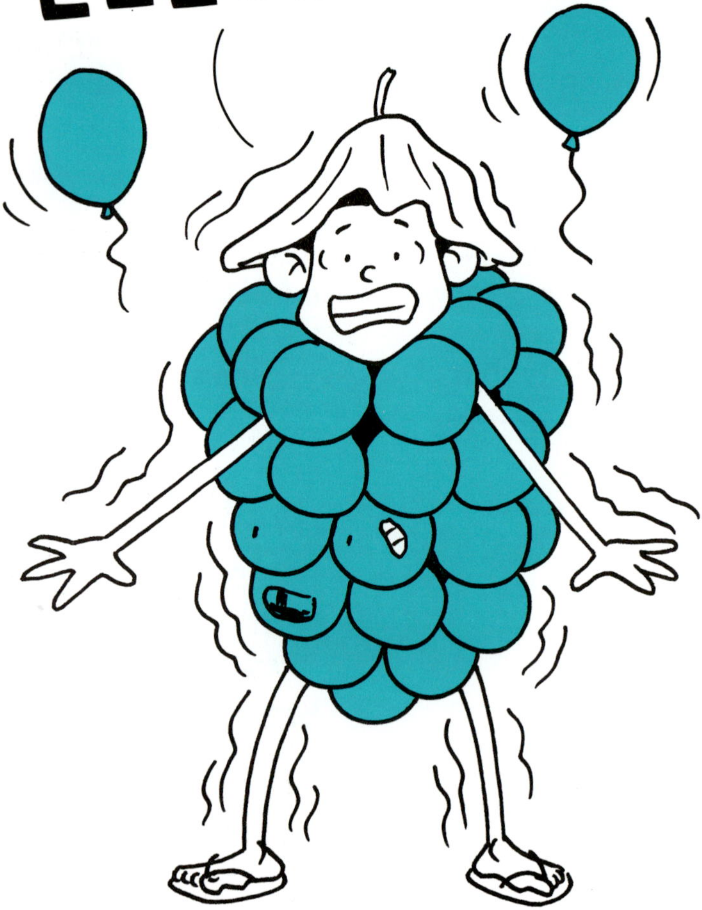

We opened the gate and walked inside. We slowly tiptoed up the path, past the long grass, overgrown weeds, and the old **FOR RENT** sign.

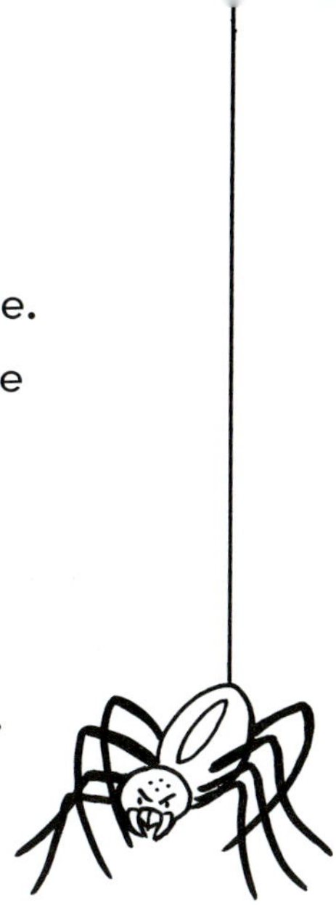

A **spider** suddenly dropped down in front of me and I **jumped** backwards.

I **tripped** over a rock

and

fell

over.

But because I was completely covered in balloons,

I hit

the

ground . . .

and **bounced right back!**

Airbags!

That was handy!

When we finally reached the door, I lifted my hand and knocked.

I hoped whoever, or **whatever**, was in there liked grapes . . .

When nobody answered, I turned to go . . . but I knew we couldn't leave **Blockhead** behind!

Just then, we heard Blockhead cry out from inside. He was **calling** to me!

WEIRDO!

WEIRDO!

Slowly, and bravely, I pushed the door open. It **creaked** really loudly, but not as loudly as the thumping of my heart!

THUMP!
THUMP!
THUMP!

I was **terrified**, but we had to **rescue Blockhead!**

We ducked under huge cobwebs and walked inside.

In the light of the moon, we saw Blockhead sitting on a couch next to **another parrot!**

GO AWAY!

GO AWAY!

SQUAWK!

DO NOT ENTER!

The creepy voice we'd heard earlier belonged to the **PARROT!** A talking parrot with a broken wing!

The parrot was telling us to **go away**, but she looked perfectly happy to see us!

At the same time, me and Bella remembered something!

'Molly? Is that you?' we asked.

MOLLY!

CHAPTER 8

We carried Blockhead and Molly next door to Bella's house, then we **found** the phone number on the **missing poster** and called **Molly's owner**.

She was **so relieved** to hear that we'd found her bird!

She turned up at Bella's house within **minutes!**

The lady and Molly even **looked alike!**

'Hello, **my little Molly!**' said the lady.

'You see,' she explained. 'I live in a house with a yard that was too small for a **guard dog**. So I got a **guard parrot** instead! I trained Molly to say things like **GO AWAY** and **DO NOT ENTER!**'

'She's a **perfectly lovely** bird,' said the lady, giving **Molly** a cuddle. 'She actually **loves** company.'

It felt **so good** to help Molly find her way back home . . . and it was **awesome** to have solved the mystery of the **spooky voice** in the **haunted house** . . .

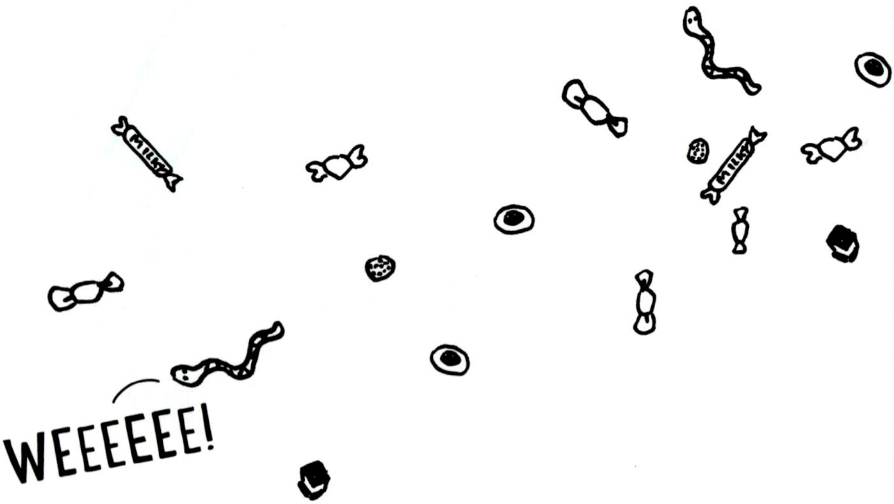

. . . a house that wasn't so **HAUNTED** after all . . .

I **ran home** to tell

Mum and Dad

all about it.

NEW FRIENDS!

CHAPTER 9

Mum and Dad went to look at the **NOT HAUNTED** house the very next day. After a few **quick calls** and a few **big talks** . . .

. . . we decided to **RENT IT!**

We didn't have to move away, after all! We only needed to move **down the street!**

And **best of all** . . . we didn't have to **change schools**!

We all love our **new house**. It's a bit **rundown** in places . . .

. . . and you can get **lost** in the **wild yard** . . .

But there's nothing we can't work around!

And one of the **coolest** things?

The house even has an **attic!**

I thought we were going to find **spiderwebs** and **dark, spooky corners** . . .

but you **won't** believe it . . .

The attic

was

filled

with . . .

BEAN BAGS!
BOING!

WEEEEEEEEE!
AHHH . . .

Blockhead has a **new friend**, who comes over to visit in the afternoons, now that her wing has healed.

And it turns out her owner – **Miss Lovely** – lives just behind us! She and Granddad **love chatting** over the fence! She thinks he's **really funny.**

It's **awesome** that Blockhead and Granddad have made **new** friends.

But I think **I'm** the **luckiest** one of all.

My **new neighbour** is just the

BEST!

FROM ANH

For Nicole–

the **best** designer!

ACKNOWLEDGEMENTS

FROM JULES

For everyone who loves to draw. Don't ever stop.

AUSTRALIAN BOOK INDUSTRY AWARDS WINNER!

Book 1

GOT IT!

bird

Book 2

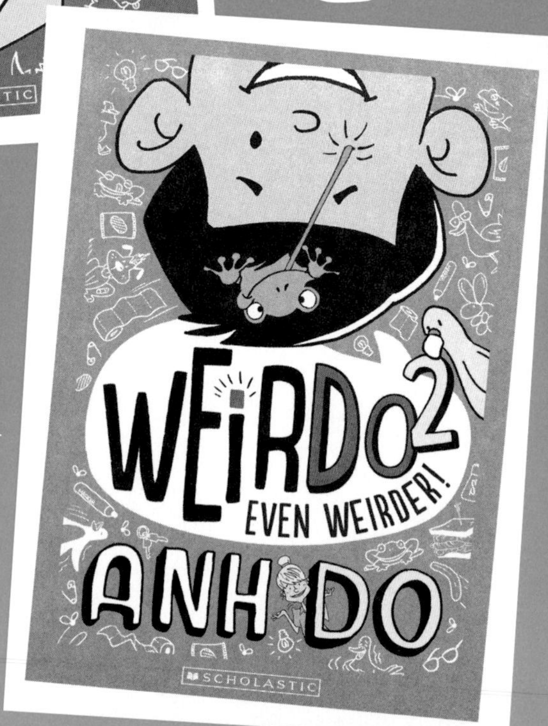

GOT IT!

COLLECT THEM ALL!

Book 3

GOT IT!

COLLECT THEM ALL!

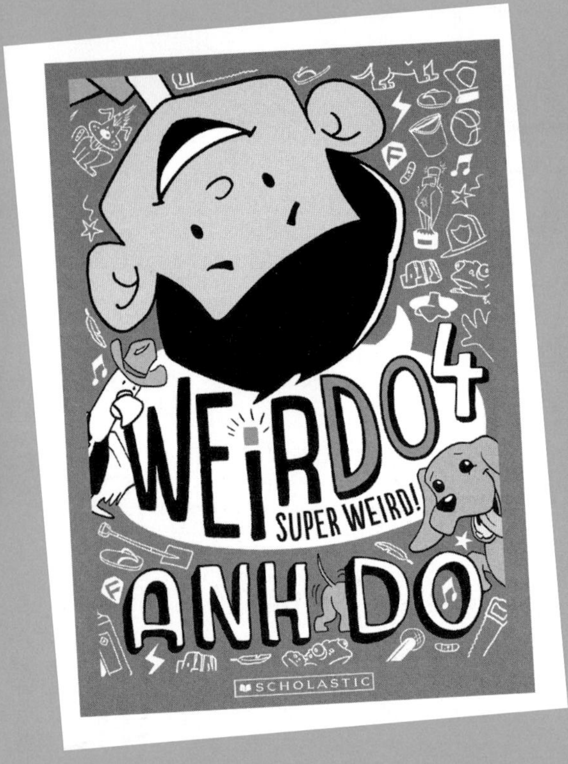

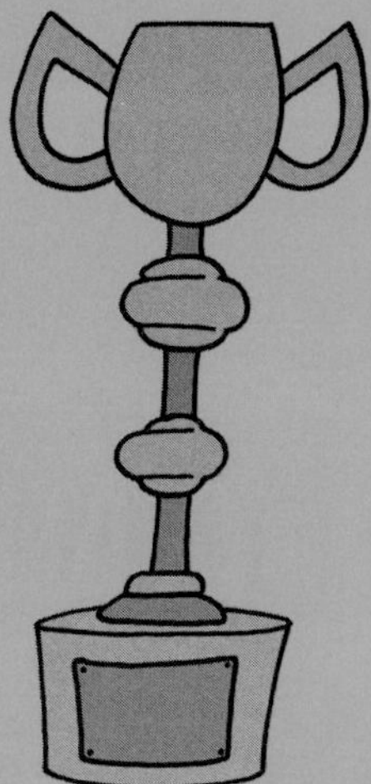

trophy

Book 4

GOT IT!

pet rock

pineapple

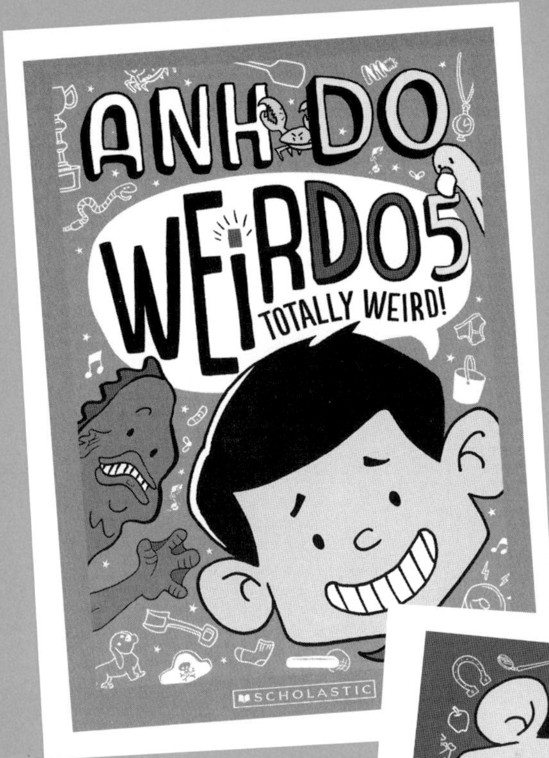

Book 5

GOT IT!

Book 6

GOT IT!

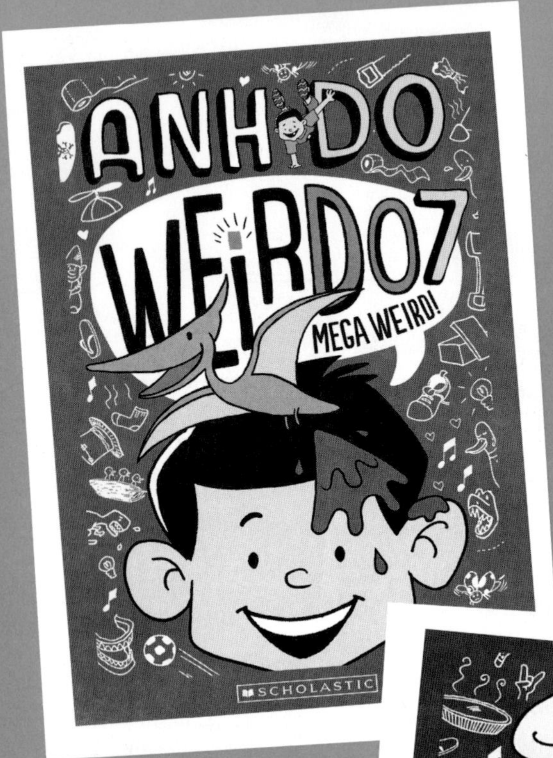

Book 7

GOT IT!

Book 8

GOT IT!

COLLECT THEM ALL!
YOU CAN NEVER HAVE TOO MANY WEIRDOS
ANH DO
WEiRDO 9
SPOOKY WEIRD!
SCHOLASTIC
Book 9
GOT IT!
pie
Roger
dino bone!

STAY
TUNED!